AF483634

Tiger and Elsa: a Royal Friendship

Cat Mama Librarian's Cats, Book 6

Brenda S. Parris

Tiger and Elsa: a Royal Friendship
Cat Mama Librarian's Cats, Book 6
Copyright © 2026 Brenda S. Parris

All rights reserved. No part of this book may be reproduced, stored in a retrieval system in any form or by any means, electronic, mechanical, photocopying, recording, or otherwise, without written permission of the publisher, except where permitted by law.
To request permissions, contact the author at bsp055@yahoo.com or sign the guestbook at https://www.zarcrom.com/users/yeartorem

ISBN: 9798994947180 (paperback)
Back Home Books
Decatur, Alabama
backhomebooks.info
brendasparris.com

Illustrations done by the author
using ChatGPT, Canva, and Fotor

In memory of
Angel,
because she was almost
all white, almost like Elsa
--Tiger

Hi! This is Tiger again.
In case you haven't met me,
I'm a long skinny gray tabby.
I've told my story before,
and Elsa has told hers,
but this one is ours together.

When Mom adopted Cocoa and me,
he and I were buddies,
but about a year later,
Misty came along.

Cocoa and Misty are both black cats.
Cocoa is a big short-haired cat,
and Misty is small and has long hair,
and a very fluffy tail.

I don't know just when it happened,
but suddenly Cocoa was
Misty's buddy instead of mine.
They cuddle up together a lot,
and they both sleep
with Mom every night.

I was pretty lonely
for a couple years,
even with Mom and
two other cats in our house.

Then came Elsa,
a solid white blue-eyed cat.
She had her own room
for almost a year,
but three stacked gates
couldn't keep me out.
I can jump high, you know.

When Mom started taking
the gates down,
she just let me come
and go as I pleased.
I would visit Elsa
several times a day,
just for a few minutes
at a time.

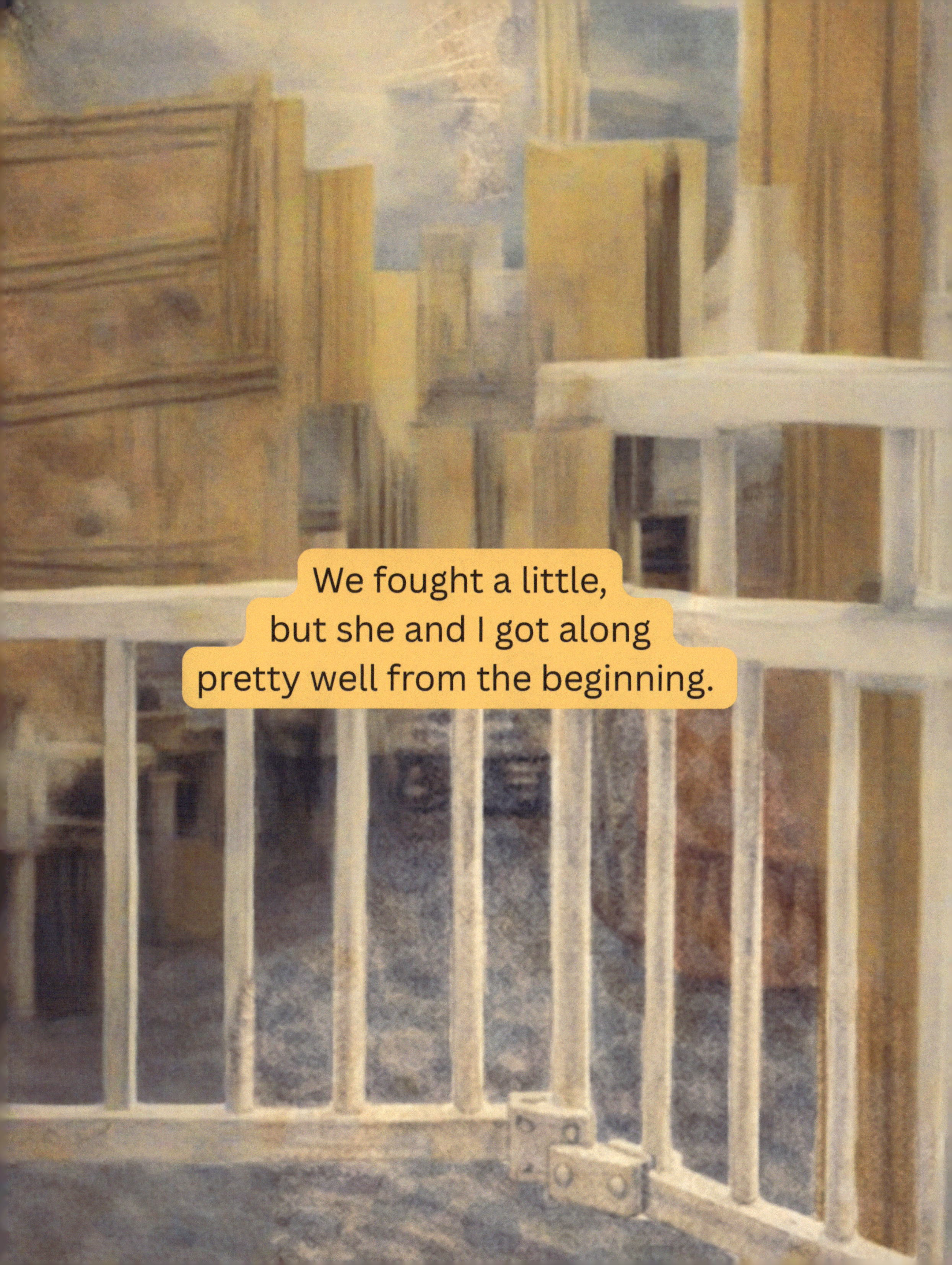
We fought a little,
but she and I got along
pretty well from the beginning.

Even before I could go in her room,
I would just stare at her.
Mom said, "You think she's
the prettiest thing you've ever seen,
don't you?"
And I answered, "Yes".

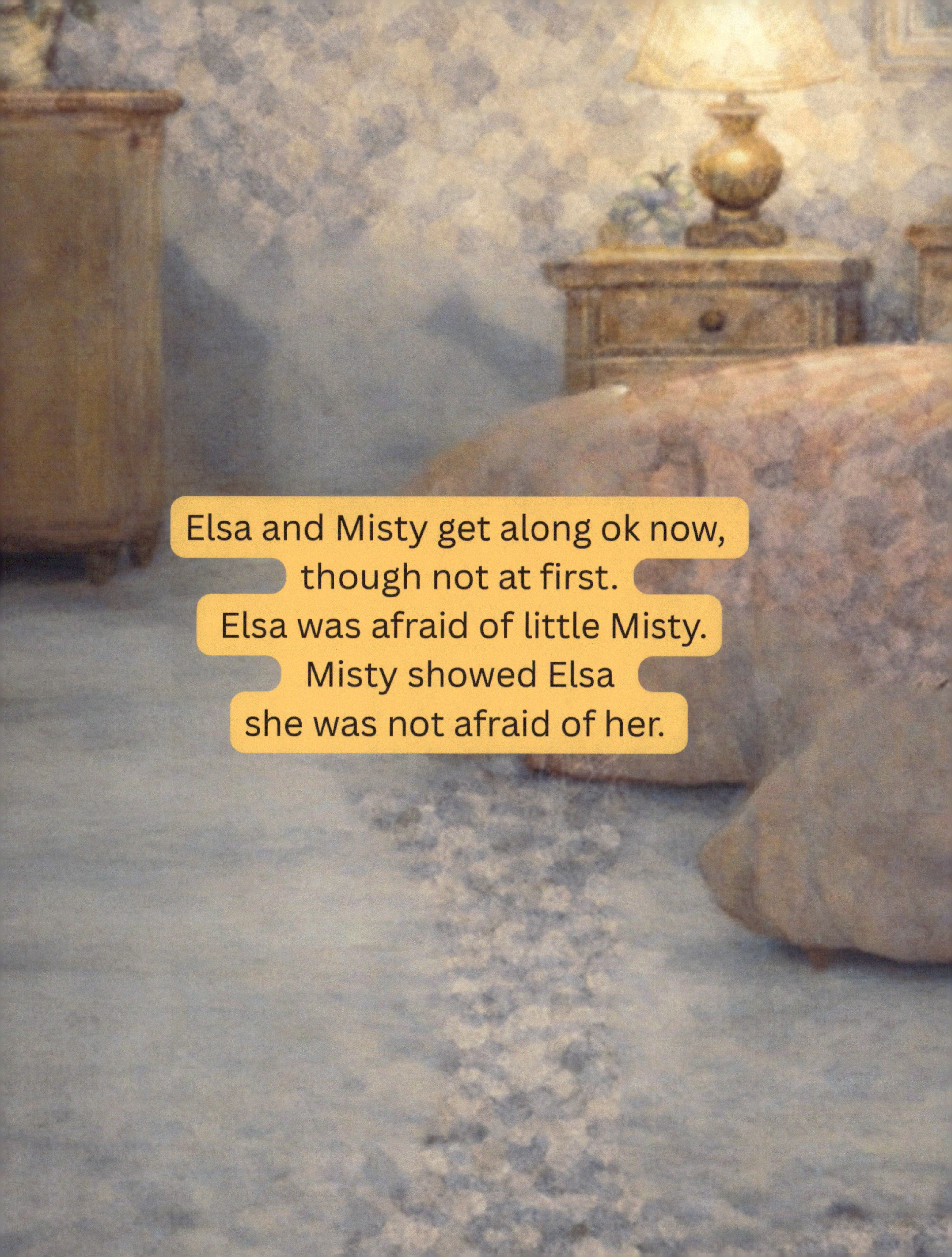
Elsa and Misty get along ok now,
though not at first.
Elsa was afraid of little Misty.
Misty showed Elsa
she was not afraid of her.

Big Cocoa is still afraid of Elsa.
I think Elsa is jealous of Cocoa.
Mom calls him her sweet gentle giant.

After Elsa moved to the living room,
I could visit her more often.
We are buddies now.

QUEEN OF THE
LIVING ROOM

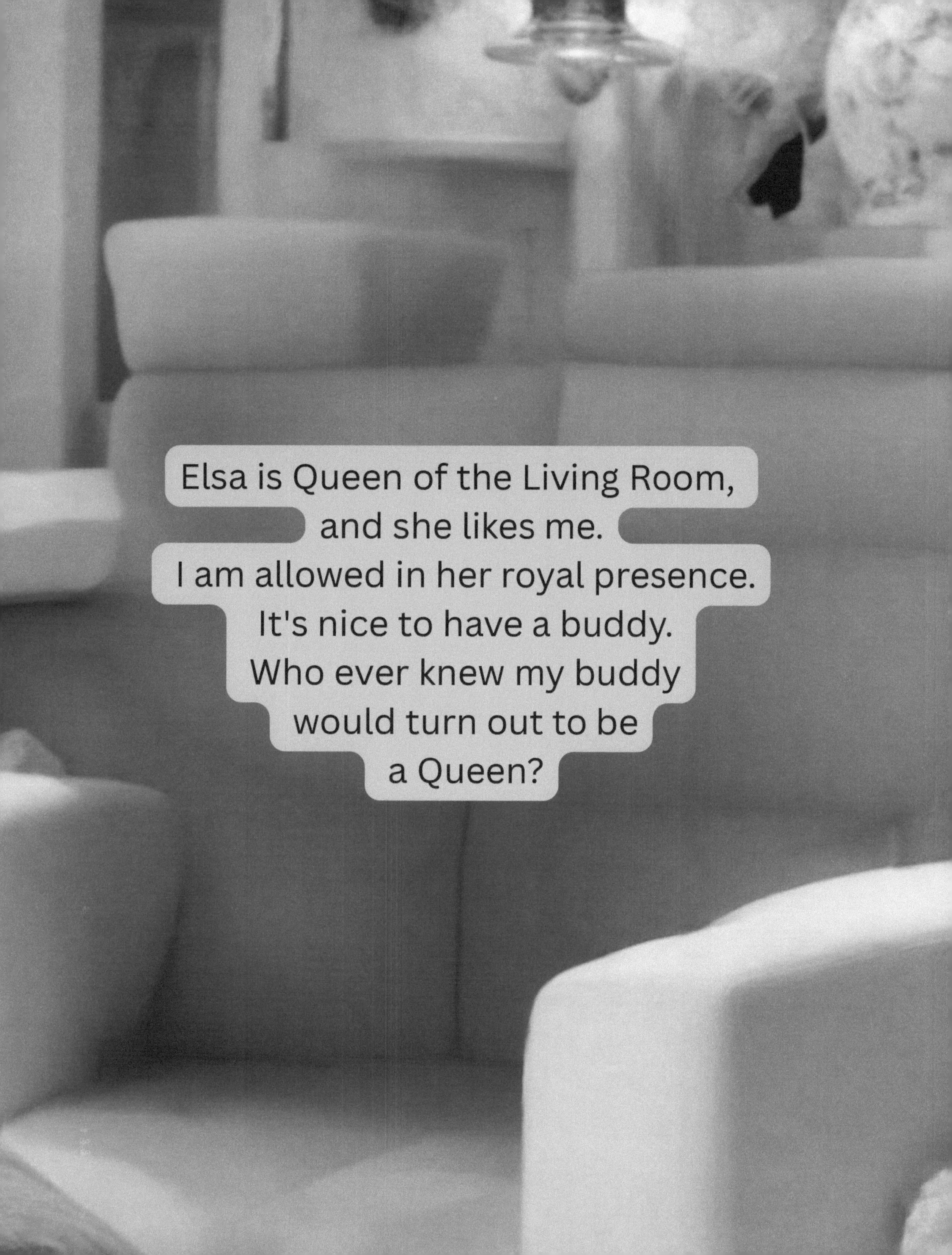
Elsa is Queen of the Living Room,
and she likes me.
I am allowed in her royal presence.
It's nice to have a buddy.
Who ever knew my buddy
would turn out to be
a Queen?

www.ingramcontent.com/pod-product-compliance
Lightning Source LLC
Chambersburg PA
CBHW041633110726
48005CB00002B/584